AF265494

The Case for Economic Nationalism

by

John Tyndall

The A.K. Chesterton Trust

2012

This booklet was first published by the National Front in 1975.

This edition is *The A.K. Chesterton Trust Reprint Series* No. 5

Printed & Published in 2012.

ISBN: 978-0-9564669-5-2

© **The A.K. Chesterton Trust, BM Candour, London, WC1N 3XX, United Kingdom.**

Website: www.candour.org.uk

Foreword

John Tyndall will need no introduction to British Nationalists.

This booklet was originally published in 1975, and provided Tyndall a relatively rare foray into Economics. Thirty five years on there is little education being provided for today's generation of Nationalists, and it is often necessary to look to the past for answers.

Although some aspects of the text are very dated, much does stand the test of time and with the world economy in tatters, who knows? The time may yet come when aspects of it can be put into practise.

Renewed links with the old dominions certainly looks an attractive possibility with the potential failure of the European Union looming.

We can only hope that someday, a free and independent Britain can be re-established.

Colin Todd

The A.K. Chesterton Trust
August 2012

This booklet is respectfully dedicated to the late John Tyndall.

Contents

<u>INTRODUCTION</u>

Economic decline has cast its shadow over Britain for so long that it cannot any more be considered as a transient phase brought on by the policies of a particular government. It has attained a status of semi-permanence in British life, with only the very oldest amongst us being able to remember any other condition. Britain entered the Seventies with one of the lowest growth rates among the developed nations. Before that she had struggled through the Sixties and was never really economically secure during the Fifties. One might be prompted to say that we are in a decline dating from our failure to recover from the last war, until on deeper examination it is realised that we never really recovered from the previous war. In fact we are dealing with a condition so deep-rooted as to reduce to irrelevance the inter-party debate on the subject which rages daily in Parliament and Press. The policies of Conservatism and Socialism have had ample opportunity during the last half-century to prove themselves in the economic field, and neither party has succeeded in bringing our decline to a halt or in really laying the foundations for economic survival in the modern world.

Were the British a technically backward race, not distinguished by any particular role in the industrial progress of Mankind, we might be forced to acknowledge that these failures were an endemic feature of the national character rather than failures of leadership and policy. But with our record of science, technology and invention and our heritage of skills and knowledge no such excuse could stand up to a moment's examination. Leadership and policy it is indeed that is at the root of our troubles, and leadership and policy in the most fundamental aspects.

The National Front, instead of restricting itself to criticism in detail of the economic programmes of recent governments, has penetrated to the very heart of the framework of British economic life and challenged some of the most basic assumptions on which it is built, the following two in particular:—

(a) That Britain's economic existence is inextricably bound up with the flow of international trade (meaning in this context with foreign countries) and depends on her ability to maintain her place as a major competitor in foreign markets.

(b) That monetary policy with regard to the creation of investment and purchasing power within the British economy must be related to the international position of the Pound and must thereby determine the powers of production rather than be determined by them. These and other assumptions are examined in a series of studies conducted by the National Front Policy Committee, and our study here is concerned particularly with (a).

The National Front is unique among political parties in Britain today in being a party of Nationalism — as opposed to Internationalism, seeking to ensure our country's future by a determined policy of national strength and self-reliance rather than by a dependence on the fragile structure of international relationships. In economic matters its doctrines correspond very closely to that principle. They aim, in a sentence, to make the British people the masters, as near as possible, of all the economic factors that govern their survival, prosperity and standard of life. As such they reject the principle fundamental to the orthodox policies of the day: that national action in the economic field must be circumscribed by world economic conditions.

<u>BREAKDOWN OF THE OLD SYSTEM</u>

THE ROOT OF THE TROUBLE

"We can get a fairly stable level of home prices if we choose, by so 'managing' our currency and credit as to keep their volume at a fairly constant ratio to the volume of things needing to be bought and sold. This is a clear and intelligible policy, which has many powerful advocates. But we can do this under present conditions only if we remain off the gold standard, and allow the value of our currency in terms of other currencies to fluctuate with changes in the level of world prices. The reason for reluctance to do this is that it is most desirable to promote world economic co-operation and exchange, and to thwart the powerful influences at present making all over the world for economic nationalism and hostility between nations. Unstable exchanges mean unstable trading relationships; and a currency so managed as to stabilize internal prices removes the possibility of working towards a single world currency, valid in every country. It is therefore a serious matter to throw over an international standard permanently, in favour of the policy of stabilizing internal prices."

THE CRISIS (Ernest Bevin and G. D. H. Cole)

The foregoing words were written in the 1930s in a climate of galloping inflation, just as now. They exhibit perfectly the thinking that has obstructed every effort to solve Britain's economic problems by firm national measures. Only one thing has altered to affect the situation since then: Britain's position in world markets is now substantially weaker and so the consequences of being tied to the world economy are that much the worse.

Britain is paying the penalty today for living with the same structure of industry and trade as she did when she was the only major manufacturing nation in the world and every country was anxious to buy her goods to the point of offering the most favourable terms of exchange. In fact this position has been steadily disappearing for at least half a century, and we are now merely one of a growing number of industrialised powers trying to sell in a world market in which competition is getting more and more intense every year. As an illustration of how we have lost ground in the world market for manufactured products, figures produced by the National Institute of Economic and Social Research show that between 1953 and 1969 Britain's share in this market declined from 21.0 percent to 11.0 percent.

Despite these trends, the prevailing economic mood of Westminster, whether on Left or Right, has assumed as an article of faith that no way out of our troubles exists except through the massive increase of our foreign exports. In view of the obvious loss of ground in traditional markets, this philosophy has taken on the form of an almost fairytale belief that the ground can be gained in new markets, hence the frantic rush to pour money into the hitherto "underdeveloped countries" in the hope that the economies of the latter will be built up to the point where they become vast consumers of British goods. But even this policy is doomed to frustration, and for a number of reasons.

In the first place it assumes that the prior requirement for the development of a country's economy is financial capital and not indigenous reserves of human energy and intelligence, whereas in fact the very opposite is the case. Where the human attributes for economic progress are lacking no amount of money will create progress.

In the second place, even where growth in the underdeveloped countries does occur there is absolutely no assurance that markets will be given to us on a basis of preference in return for services rendered. We are pursued in these new markets by the same cut- throat international competition that has forced us out of older ones, often to the point where native buyers play one would-be supplier off against another with the result that all lose except the buyers themselves.

A third factor against us is the nascent industry of the newly developed countries themselves. Those countries that have what it takes to develop economically are bound in the course of time to represent new competitors not only within their own markets but in world markets. As fast as markets expand, so does the competition to supply them.

CHEAP LABOUR THREAT

A further factor affecting our ability to sell in world markets has arisen with ominous force during recent years. Vast industrial concerns based in the older manufacturing countries have started to set up plant in many underdeveloped lands and employ cheap local labour in the making of cut-price products. In this way the German Rollei-Werke recently decided to invest £5 million in a new plant to make cameras in Singapore, where wage rates are only one-sixth of those in Germany itself. The American Signetics Corporation flies components to South Korea, where workers assemble them into integrated circuits that are flown back to the U.S., to be fitted into computers. It pays off. The Korean workers are paid 45 dollars a month as against the 350 dollars that would have to be paid to the company's workers in California.

The potential of this threat is awesome to contemplate. The type of cheap labour involved is eminently suited to the drudgery of automated mass-production that the work entails. In the international trading jungle it has a head start against the relatively highly paid workers of Western countries, including those of Britain.

Meanwhile we are confronted with yet another form of competition against which we cannot hope to survive except by undermining our whole standard of life. Industry behind the Iron Curtain is dumping goods in non-communist countries at prices often below cost. It can do this because it is subject to none of the profit-and-loss laws that govern normal economic intercourse as we know it. The loss is borne by the workers themselves, who go chronically short of normal consumer goods, and because of the kind of State under which they live they have no option but to bear their fate in silence. Soviet and other communist industry engages in this practice because its primary purpose in exporting is not commercial but political. It means to cause havoc in the economies of countries that are marked out for red penetration, and will go to any expense to achieve that object including slave labour conditions for its own people.

It must surely be seen that the cumulative effect of these forces at work in the world economy is to make mincemeat of any illusions that an economic revival can be achieved in Britain by means of some spectacular future growth in our share of world trade. It is perfectly true that numerous internal conditions within Britain itself, such as inept management and industrial unrest, represent factors which, if corrected, would improve our prospects in world markets for a time, but this would not alter the basic trend of international economics, which is that the world's manufacturing capacity is developing in excess of its power to consume, and that the success of one exporter can only be achieved through the failure of another — leading the latter to keep wages down in order to recover its competitiveness, and a resultant vicious circle of undercutting in which the standard of life of ordinary people is continually kept down at a level far below that which the power of science now makes possible.

THE ALTERNATIVE

PRODUCING FOR THE HOME MARKET

As a reaction against the madness of the international system, and opposed to the whole principle of *laissez faire* world economics, there has arisen during this century the alternative economic doctrine: **that industry should be organised to cater predominantly for the home market — with export trade an agreeable bonus rather than the sole means of survival.** This doctrine, unlike that of Messrs. Bevin and Cole and the whole school of leftist and liberal theorists, does not see international exchange of goods as a desirable end for its own sake; it sees it as a necessity for certain nations that have a substantial shortage of one product and/or a substantial surplus of another. The extent to which each nation must be committed to international trade varies, of course, from one to another depending on diversity of resources and structure of industry, but obviously the greatest advantage lies with those nations that are committed the least to the world market and reliant to the maximum on the home market. To aim at such a position is what we understand by economic nationalism.

At this point it is interesting to examine two great industrial powers which both to a degree have pursued such a course, the United States and Japan.

Those who think of the United States as a major participant in international trade today should not overlook the fact that that country's foreign trade still represents a comparatively minor part of her total business and only seems large because of the immensity of the American economy as a whole. In recent years the Americans have become more involved in the world's business than previously and this has certainly been to their detriment since it has exposed the American market to a huge flood of foreign imports.

However, if we look back at the development of the American economy during that period in which it advanced from pastoral beginnings to that of representing the world's top industrial power we will see that the process represented an almost classic case of economic nationalism in operation. Perhaps circumstance rather than State policy was the prime motivator, for America had the advantage of so many natural resources that other countries lacked, but she was not without powerful voices in Senate and Congress, as well as in business, that applied pressure in favour of protective practices. The result was that American industry grew from the foundations of a huge and prosperous home market, and by reason of that home market was able to operate at a cost effectiveness far superior to that of industries elsewhere in the world. Under such a system overseas exports could take the form of dumping, that is the disposal of surplus production at only a fraction above cost. Such has been one of the main factors in making for America's power in world markets.

EXAMPLE OF JAPAN

Japan is a different case from America in so far as she has little of the natural resources of the latter — less in fact than Britain. Japan is forced by circumstance to be a major importer of raw materials, and this, combined with her massive inroads into world markets for manufactured goods, has led some people to place her in the same economic category as Britain, i.e. that of an itinerant world trader adhering to orthodox *laissez faire* doctrine.

Such a picture is in fact grossly misleading. The expansion of Japan's manufacturing industries has taken place behind strict protective barriers operated in a very subtle way. While Japan pays lip service to GATT, the international treaty standing for world free trade, and does not operate official embargoes or tariff charges, all manner of indirect pressures are applied against Japanese industry by a Government-appointed body known as the Ministry of International Trade and Industry — with the result that a 'Buy Japanese' policy is followed throughout the country in all produce that can be supplied from home sources.

The protection of the booming motor industry is a case in point. In recent years the growth of this industry has contrasted vividly with the stagnation of our own, and it is a matter of great interest to discover the source of its growth from an annual output of **less than 400** cars in 1948 to 2½ **million** in 1970. In fact about 80 percent of the latter figure are sold in Japan, whilst barely half of the 1¾ million cars produced annually in Britain are sold in Britain. The growth of the Japanese car industry is based on the tremendous strength of the home market. The same procedure has occurred in other industries. As a report in the London *Observer* records, "The Japanese assault on world markets was not unplanned. Japanese cameras, radios and automobiles made a sudden and dazzling appearance, one by one, on the world market as if they had sprung from nowhere. In fact they were developed on the Japanese home market, protected from any sort of foreign competition, until the volume of production brought costs down and quality up to the point where the Japanese article was a strong competitor on world markets. Only then did Sony, Nikon, Toyota and the rest burst forth. Next on the list, according to plan is the Japanese computer."

From these examples we see that America and Japan, in their different ways, have been governed in vital growth periods by a form of economic thinking that is essentially nationalist. The one has the fortunate asset of immense natural resources to assist her policies. The other lacks that asset but has followed a policy of national self-interest and self-containment to the limit that her resources have allowed. America and Japan are respectively the first and third most powerful industrial nations in the world today, and the latter may before long replace Russia as the second.

STRENGTHENING THE BRITISH MARKET

The National Front has urged that for Britain to realise the full economic strength that her native skills permit she must turn away from internationalism and towards a policy that aims at much greater self-sufficiency.

When the matter of Britain's huge commitment to imports and exports is discussed, it is often assumed that this is made inevitable by the limitations of our natural resources and that we have to export on the scale we do in order to import the goods we cannot produce ourselves. **In fact, if we break down imports into their three basic categories we will find that approximately 30 percent consist of raw materials, another 30 percent of food products and no less than 40 percent of manufactured goods!** It is largely a fallacy, therefore, to believe that we are all the time importing products that we cannot obtain from home sources; this is only partially true.

There is absolutely no major field of manufacturing in which the skills do not exist, or at least cannot be quickly developed, for Britain to produce to satisfy all her own needs. As evidence has shown, Japan created great industries from scratch to produce such commodities as cameras — which we import on a large scale — by a determined national policy enforced by protective measures. We can do the same — as we can do with typewriters, transistor radios, computers, watches, printing equipment, aircraft and the many categories of armaments that we buy from all over the world. Needless to say, there is also no type of motor vehicle that British manufacturers cannot supply in the highest quality, given full access to the home market. There is no reason at all why our imports of finished goods should not be reduced to just a tiny number of specialities and the enormous volume of trade involved switched to home industries with a consequent revitalisation all round.

REVIVAL OF AGRICULTURE

In the case of food imports, massive savings could again be made. Robert Hart, the distinguished authority on farming, forestry and conservation, has said in his book, *The Inviolable Hills:* "By a large scale upland reclamation drive combined with an intensive effort by the urban population comparable to the 'dig for victory' campaign of the last war, the people of Britain could make a major contribution to the balance of payments problem and the world food crisis — if they had the will.

"The British hills, with their climate ameliorated by afforestation and their soils made fertile and absorptive by organic cultivation and conservation practices, could produce a far wider range of agricultural products with much greater intensity than today."

The opinions of experts vary as to the extent to which Britain could achieve self-sufficiency in food requirements, but there is unanimous agreement that we could provide substantially more of our own food than is at present the case, thus not only reducing our expenditure on imported products but also rendering ourselves less vulnerable to blockade in times of war.

Where raw materials are concerned there are fields in which human ingenuity — which we certainly do not lack as a nation — can devise substitutes, and new discoveries of oil and natural gas in the North Sea region may go a long way towards meeting some of our fuel requirements. However, it is not denied that in this category of goods a major part of our supplies must still be obtained from overseas.

It must be understood that in opposing the principle of economic internationalism with that of national self-sufficiency we are dealing in matters of degree. Absolutes of either one or the other are out of the question, and when we speak of self-sufficiency we are speaking not of an economy living in watertight insulation from the rest of the world but one which strives for the maximum reliance on home resources that can be obtained with reasonable economy.

REBUILDING COMMONWEALTH TRADE

ENLARGING THE MARKET

In making Britain more self-reliant, it is obvious that there are limits on what can be achieved in an island territory with an area of 94,000 square miles and a population of a little under sixty millions. We should try to reach nearer to those limits but we should recognise them where they exist. Because of them Britain alone cannot possibly aspire to the economic resourcefulness of super powers like America. To approach the potential of the American economy, Britain must have access to a large market beyond her shores. How can such a market be obtained in which we can enjoy protected rights and not be exposed as we are now to the international cut-price jungle?

This question has been asked by economists and politicians on whom the lessons of our failure to maintain our old dominance in world export markets have not been lost. Unfortunately, it has been answered all too often by incursion into fantasy as great as that from which it seeks to escape. The substitute fantasy is the European Common Market.

The European Common Market does not possess the means to achieve the conditions of either America or Japan. It cannot achieve the conditions of America because, like our own island economy, it does not possess the natural resources of America. The European nations, whether operating individually or collectively, still have to import from outside Europe most of their raw materials and therefore still have to find markets outside Europe for a large part of their manufactured produce. Nor can Europe achieve the conditions of

Japan because to do so would mean getting half her factories to close down in order to rationalise production, and while that might be distantly possible (to the sacrifice of huge numbers of workers) in a single country where an element of national unity prevailed, it is quite impossible in a conglomeration of countries where national interests are certain to conflict in the process.

The idea of the European Economic Community is not, in fact, a departure from internationalist thinking; it is merely a variant of internationalist thinking, and its driving force lies much more in a doctrinaire commitment to internationalism as an end in itself than in any reasoned appreciation of economic laws or facts.

However, there is a practical means by which British industry can expand in a larger market without massive exposure to the contortions of the cut-price world economy.

COMMONWEALTH PREFERENCE

The National Front has urged from its beginning a re-dedication in Britain to the institution of Commonwealth, and in doing so it has been careful to distinguish between the Old Commonwealth, as an association based on kinship and shared interests and values, and the present multi-racial Commonwealth, which has no unifying elements and which to Britain today represents more of a burden than an asset. We have reiterated time and again that the latter concept of Commonwealth and the illusions attending it should be abandoned, but that we should seek to preserve and strengthen the Commonwealth where it involves peoples of British origin.

Elsewhere in our policy series we have proposed how a new political structure might be devised for the Commonwealth which would respect the local sovereignty of its members but lead to a greater acting together in world affairs. Here we are concerned purely with economic aspects.

Canada, Australia and New Zealand are countries which are of first consideration when we think of family ties with Britain. These ties have been allowed to become weaker in recent decades and trading links, once very firm, have become loosened, but this has not been so much a natural process as the outcome of neglect by successive British governments and in particular of the recent orientation of British policy towards Europe.

In point of fact, every pretext that has been advanced to support the idea of an economic community embracing Britain and Europe can be applied with doubled strength in advocating an economic community of the Old Commonwealth. If there is an element of affinity between Britons and the Continental Europeans, there is a far greater element of affinity between Britons and the inhabitants of the Dominions. If it be said that in joining Europe Britain is linking herself to economies that are growing faster than her own, then it may be answered that the Dominions have economies that are growing much faster than those of Europe. In fifty years time the nations of the Old Commonwealth will be three, four or more times their present size and indeed Australia and Canada, with their vast territories and resources, can expand almost indefinitely. On the other hand it is clear that most of the European nations are near to the limit of their size and development.

COMPLEMENTARY ECONOMIES

But the vital fact which overrides all else so far as economic considerations are concerned is this: Britain and the Old Commonwealth have nearly complementary economies. The Commonwealth countries are primary producers on a large scale, and despite recent industrialisation will always remain so by virtue of their natural situation and assets. Britain is and will remain principally a secondary producer, even if efforts are made at greater cultivation of farming and raw materials. Her natural situation and assets make no other course conceivable. **It is by joining complementary economies (and not competitive ones, such as those of Europe) that the advantages of a larger market are obtained.**

Australia, New Zealand and Canada are countries perfectly fitted to provide most of Britain's important needs. Canada is the world's largest producer of nickel and its second largest producer of aluminium. In addition, she has great reserves of copper, zinc, iron, gold, silver, lead, platinum, cobalt, tungsten, magnesium, uranium, petroleum and timber. Australia produces coal, zinc, iron, lead, copper, gold, uranium, nickel and bauxite, as well as being, like Canada, a leading supplier of well known farming products. The great contribution of New Zealand to our needs in dairy products is well known.

It would be the policy of the National Front to negotiate the formation of a common trading bloc between these countries and Britain, as well as South Africa and Rhodesia, now at present outside the Commonwealth but associated with it by long tradition. We would seek, in effect, something very similar to the Common Market structure now being sought with Europe, that is to say a market with the minimum of tariff barriers between its members but with tariff barriers against goods from outside. This may not be possible to achieve in its entirety but to achieve it to a substantial degree would be of enormous benefit to Britain and indeed to her partners.

We realise that the spontaneous acceptance of a Commonwealth trading bloc is not something that we can take for granted in the countries concerned. A great deal of diplomacy, coupled with real proof of our intention to support our partners in trade, will be needed.

Australia and New Zealand offer in these respects a less difficult prospect than Canada, and it may well be that we would have to pursue agreements with the countries of the Antipodes and make them work for some time before our Atlantic cousins would wish to enter the partnership.

Where agricultural products are concerned, we believe that it would be unwise to pursue greater self-sufficiency in the United Kingdom in cases where the result would be to diminish the market for Commonwealth suppliers. Our drive to increase home production should be directed at the expense of foreign suppliers.

In advocating a Commonwealth economic community we have stressed very strongly our belief that natural elements, such as kinship and complementary economic resources, are in the long run of much greater import than current trends in politics or trade. The latter are alterable whereas the former are not. It is perfectly true that current political and trading trends pose barriers to the unity of the Old Commonwealth that are greater than they were ten, twenty or thirty years ago, **but these are still much less than the thousand-year-old barriers that separate the nations now being expected to form a united Europe**, to say nothing of the irreconcilable economic interests of those nations which Common Market negotiations have highlighted. We are not proposing a smooth and easy path where reconsolidation of the Old Commonwealth is concerned, only an objective that is more feasible and more acceptable than any other open to us.

MARKET OF 100 MILLION

The Commonwealth trading area proposed would represent a combined population of nearly 100 millions, with an average purchasing power per head considerably higher than that of the

United Kingdom as at present. This would mean a doubling of the home market, but, much more important, British industry would be able to operate in this size of market without the corresponding inroads by other manufacturers into the U.K. market that would result from our entering Europe. This is not to ignore the young and growing manufacturing industries in the Dominions but only to state that they represent a mere fraction of the industrial capacity of Germany, France, Italy and the Low Countries.

This point must be underlined: we do not, as did the older imperialists, expect the Dominions just to be Britain's farmyard and supplier of minerals. We expect them to strive, in their own interests, to develop their domestic sources of secondary production — as they are indeed doing. However, equally in their own interests, they are going to continue to capitalise on their natural resources, which are far greater than those of Europe, so that it is always certain that a lesser portion of their economy will be devoted to manufacturing than in our part of the world. This creates the basis for a natural trading relationship between us.

And looking ahead, as we must do, it must be repeated that the next half century will see a far greater growth in Commonwealth markets than is possible in the markets of Europe.

As has been said with Britain, it must also be said with the Commonwealth as a whole that the building of a powerfully fortified home market does not preclude a very considerable trade with the world as a whole. Britain in secondary products, and the Commonwealth countries in primary products, have a very large surplus capacity that must be sold in world markets. In the course of time it should be hoped that Commonwealth members can be persuaded more and more to restructure their economies so as to cater for internal needs, but a substantial foreign trade will always be necessary. Our policy simply means that British and Commonwealth producers will participate in international trade from the base of an immensely strong home market, which, like that of America, will allow a scale of production that will make our position in international trade much more competitive and at the same time greatly increase our economic independence.

It may finally be asked: supposing by the time you were in a position to pursue these policies Britain was a signatory to the Treaty of Rome and firmly in the Common Market. We can only answer that we shall never recognise the validity of a British signature to the Rome Treaty that is not supported by a majority of the British people — as certainly no signature in the foreseeable future will be. We would therefore repudiate the Treaty and withdraw Britain from Europe.

THE ETHOS OF SELF-SUFFICIENCY

It is perhaps appropriate to conclude this study with a word about the moral aspect of a system which aims at greater self-sufficiency in the economy. Many fashionable political philosophers of the last half-century admit, like those quoted earlier, the economic common sense of a national system but repudiate it because it runs contrary to the drive towards 'world unity' that is the modern obsession. We would immediately reject the assertion that a Government has an obligation to comply with this abstract concept that overrides its duty to care for the well-being of its own people. However, even were such a concept accepted, it is a complete fiction that an intensification of international trade is an aid to world friendship and peace. On the contrary, it is the frantic rush of nations lacking their own basis for self-sustenance to sell their exports on the markets of the world that does so much to create the friction from which Mankind is suffering. Practically every historian who has analysed the causes of the First World War, for instance, has acknowledged the major part played by the stampede for world markets and in particular the rivalry in world trade between Britain and Germany.

On the other hand, a nation occupied predominantly in developing its own resources and with its reliance on export markets reduced to moderate levels is far less prone to clash with its fellow nations. Most of the strife that exists in the world today comes of one nation concerning itself overmuch with another's business. We firmly believe in minding Britain's business, and our policies in the economic field are based essentially on that belief.

About John Tyndall

John Tyndall was born Exeter, 1934. Educated Beckenham Grammar School. Played cricket (School 1st XI and Kent trialist), rugby and soccer (Kent Minor XI). Served in Royal Horse Artillery 1952-54. Began political study and activity soon after leaving forces but did not join any of the older political parties, being convinced that none of them offered the right solutions to Britain's problems. Was active in a number of patriotic and Nationalist groups, including the League of Empire Loyalists, before founding the Greater Britain Movement in 1964 and his own publishing company, Albion Press, and the magazine Spearhead at the same time. He disbanded the GBM in 1967 and with his colleagues joined the National Front. Hobbies: reading, sport and music.

John Hutchyns Tyndall (14 July 1934 - 19 July 2005).

About The A.K. Chesterton Trust

The A.K. Chesterton Trust was formed by Colin Todd and the late Miss. Rosine de Bounevialle in January 1996 to succeed and continue the work of the now defunct Candour Publishing Co.

The objects of the Trust are stated as follows:

"To promote and expound the principles of A.K. Chesterton which are defined as being to demonstrate the power of, and to combat the power of International Finance, and to promote the National Sovereignty of the British World."

Our aims include:

- *Maintaining and expanding the range of material relevant to A.K. Chesterton and his associates throughout his life.*

- *To preserve and keep in-print important works on British Nationalism in order to educate the current generation of our people.*

- *The maintenance and recovery of the sovereign independence of the British Peoples throughout the world.*

- *The strengthening of the spiritual and material bonds between the British Peoples throughout the world.*

- *The resurgence at home and abroad of the British spirit.*

We will raise funds by way of merchandising and donations.

We ask that our friends make provision for *The A.K. Chesterton Trust* in their will.

The A.K. Chesterton Trust has a **duty** to keep *Candour* in the ring and punching.

CANDOUR: To defend national sovereignty against the menace of international finance.

CANDOUR: To serve as a link between Britons all over the world in protest against the surrender of their world heritage.

<u>Subscribe to Candour</u>

CANDOUR SUBSCRIPTION RATES FOR 10 ISSUES.

U.K. £25.00
Europe 40 Euros.
Rest of the World £35.00.
USA $50.00.

All Airmail. Cheques and Postal Orders, £'s Sterling only, made payable to *The A.K. Chesterton Trust*. (Others, please send cash by **secure post**, $ bills or Euro notes.)

Payment by Paypal is available. Please see our website **www.candour.org.uk** for more information.

<u>Candour Back Issues</u>

Back issues are available. 1953 to the present.

Please request our back issue catalogue by sending your name and address with two 1st class stamps to:

The A.K. Chesterton Trust, BM Candour, London, WC1N 3XX, United Kingdom.

Alternatively, see our website at **www.candour.org.uk** where you can order a growing selection on-line.

The A.K. Chesterton Trust Reprint Series

1. Creed of a Fascist Revolutionary & Why I Left Mosley - A.K. Chesterton.

2. The Menace of World Government & Britain's Graveyard - A.K. Chesterton.

3. What You Should Know About The United Nations - The League of Empire Loyalists.

4. The Menace of the Money-Power - A.K. Chesterton.

5. The Case for Economic Nationalism - John Tyndall.

6. Sound the Alarm! - A.K. Chesterton.

7. Six Principles of British Nationalism - John Tyndall.

8. B.B.C. - A National Menace - A.K. Chesterton.

9. Stand by the Empire - A.K. Chesterton.

10. Tomorrow. A Plan for the British Future - A.K. Chesterton.

11. The British Constitution and the Corruption of Parliament - Ben Greene.

12. Very High Finance & The Policy of a Patriot - Cahill & Strasser

Other Titles from *The A.K. Chesterton Trust*

Leopard Valley – by A.K. Chesterton.

Juma The Great – by A.K. Chesterton.

The New Unhappy Lords – by A.K. Chesterton.

Facing The Abyss – by A.K. Chesterton.

The History of the League of Empire Loyalists – by H. McNeile & R. Black

The A.B.C. of Politics - by Rosine de Bounevialle

Hidden Government- by John Creagh Scott

All the above titles are available from The A.K. Chesterton Trust, BM Candour, London, WC1N 3XX, UK. (www.candour.org.uk)

www.ingramcontent.com/pod-product-compliance
Lightning Source LLC
Chambersburg PA
CBHW061106050726
47592CB00004B/1844